SYMBOLS OF AMERICA

UNCLE SAM

BY BARBARA M. LINDE

Gareth Stevens
PUBLISHING

Please visit our website, www.garethstevens.com. For a free color catalog of all our high-quality books, call toll free 1-800-542-2595 or fax 1-877-542-2596.

Library of Congress Cataloging-in-Publication Data

Names: Linde, Barbara M., author.
Title: Uncle Sam / Barbara M. Linde.
Description: New York : Gareth Stevens Publishing, [2019] | Series: Symbols of America | Includes index.
Identifiers: LCCN 2018023549| ISBN 9781538229026 (library bound) | ISBN 9781538232347 (pbk.) | ISBN 9781538232354 (6 pack)
Subjects: LCSH: Uncle Sam (Symbolic character)–Juvenile literature.
Classification: LCC E179 .L56 2019 | DDC 398.20973/02–dc23
LC record available at https://lccn.loc.gov/2018023549

Published in 2019 by
Gareth Stevens Publishing
111 East 14th Street, Suite 349
New York, NY 10003

Designer: Sarah Liddell
Editor: Joshua Turner

Photo credits: Cover, p. 1 (crumpled texture) ag1100/Shutterstock.com; cover, pp. 1, 11 (Uncle Sam) Everett Historical/Shutterstock.com; p. 5 photo courtesy of Library of Congress; p. 7 Arlo Barnes/Wikimedia Commons; p. 9 Illegitimate Barrister/Wikimedia Commons; p. 13 Historical/Contributor/Corbis Historical/ Getty Images; p. 15 SuperStock/SuperStock/Getty Images; p. 17 BotMultiChillT/ Wikimedia Commons; p. 19 MattWade/Wikimedia Commons; p. 21 KAVEBEAR/ Wikimedia Commons.

Printed in the United States of America

CPSIA compliance information: Batch #CW19GS: For further information contact Gareth Stevens, New York, New York at 1-800-542-2595.

CONTENTS

Boldface words appear in the glossary.

A Symbol of Our Country

Can a country have an uncle? Sort of. The United States has Uncle Sam. He's not a real uncle like you might have. Uncle Sam is a **symbol** of the United States government. "Uncle Sam" is also a **nickname** for the United States.

Our Country
Uncle Sam

A Real Uncle Sam?

There may have been an Uncle Sam! A meat packer named Samuel Wilson from Troy, New York, sent beef to the men during the **War of 1812**. He stamped the letters "U. S." for "United States" on the barrels. But the soldiers called it "Uncle Sam's food."

Thomas Nast's Cartoons

In the early 1800s, people began using the name "Uncle Sam" to talk about the US government. Artist Thomas Nast drew pictures of Uncle Sam. This cartoon from 1869 shows Uncle Sam serving Thanksgiving dinner. He is trying to show that Americans from all **cultures** are **equal**.

AMENDMENT
WELCOM
GRANT
CASTLE
SELF GOVERN
UNIVERSAL SUFFRAGE.

James Flagg's Idea

The United States needed soldiers to fight in **World War I**. Artist James Montgomery Flagg made a drawing of Uncle Sam for the army in 1916. He used his own face for Uncle Sam. Many people who saw the poster joined the army.

I WANT YOU
FOR U.S. ARMY
NEAREST RECRUITING STATION

Posters for World War II

Flagg drew more posters during **World War II**. Some posters asked for soldiers, nurses, or other workers. The government needed everyone to help with the war. Flagg's posters showed people how to do things like grow gardens and save money.

Uncle Sam Today

Flagg's drawing became the way Uncle Sam is shown most of the time. The army still uses Uncle Sam posters, and Uncle Sam is shown in cartoons about the government. Some people use Uncle Sam to sell cars, houses, and many other things.

DONT
WALK

Congress Honors

For more than 100 years, people heard the story that Samuel Wilson was the real Uncle Sam. Some believed it, but others didn't. In 1961, the United States **Congress** said Wilson was the real man behind Uncle Sam.

SAMUEL ★ WILSON

Uncle Sam Day

In 1989, Congress said that September 13 would always be a day to honor Samuel Wilson and Uncle Sam. This was Samuel Wilson's birthday. September 13, 1989, was also the 200th anniversary of the city of Troy, where Wilson lived.

SAMUEL WILSON'S
GRAVE IN TROY, NEW YORK

See Uncle Sam!

To this day, a lot of people dress up like Uncle Sam, such as at historic places or in parades. You can buy or make an Uncle Sam costume to wear for an event. Keep your eyes open—Uncle Sam might be close by!

GLOSSARY

Congress: the group of people who make the laws for the country

culture: the beliefs and ways of life of a group of people

equal: the same

nickname: a name different from a real name used when talking about a person or place

symbol: a picture, shape, or object that stands for something else

War of 1812: a war between the United States and Great Britain from 1812 to 1815

World War I: a war fought from 1914 to 1918 that involved countries around the world

World War II: a war fought from 1939 to 1945 that involved countries around the world

FOR MORE INFORMATION

BOOKS

Keenan, Sheila. *O, Say Can You See? America's Symbols, Landmarks, and Important Words*. New York, NY: Scholastic Nonfiction, 2007.

Monroe, Tyler. *Uncle Sam*. North Mankato, MN: Capstone Press, 2013.

WEBSITES

Wonderopolis. Wonder of the Day #527 Who Is Uncle Sam?
wonderopolis.org/wonder/who-is-uncle-sam
Listen to the text or read along to the history of Uncle Sam.

Uncle Sam: The Man and the Meme
americanhistory.si.edu/blog/2013/09/uncle-sam-the-man-and-the-meme-the-origins-of-uncle-sam.html
Read how the story of Uncle Sam started!

Publisher's note to educators and parents: Our editors have carefully reviewed these websites to ensure that they are suitable for students. Many websites change frequently, however, and we cannot guarantee that a site's future contents will continue to meet our high standards of quality and educational value. Be advised that students should be closely supervised whenever they access the internet.

INDEX